My Easter Bible

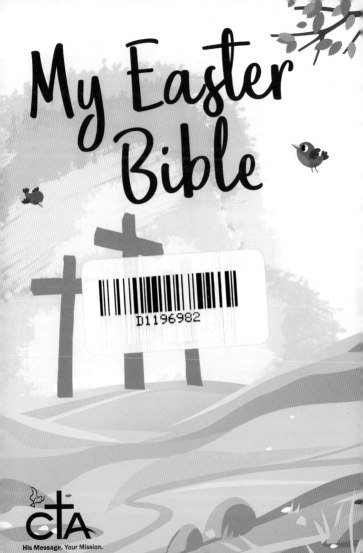

CTA
His Message. Your Mission.

The vision of CTA is
to see Christians highly effective
in their ministry so that Christ's Kingdom
is strengthened and expanded.

My Easter Bible

Copyright © 2019 CTA, Inc.
1625 Larkin Williams Rd.
Fenton, MO 63026

www.CTAinc.com

ISBN 978-1-947699-03-8
Printed for CTA, Inc. Fenton, MO 63026
Printed in Bangpakong, Thailand October 2018

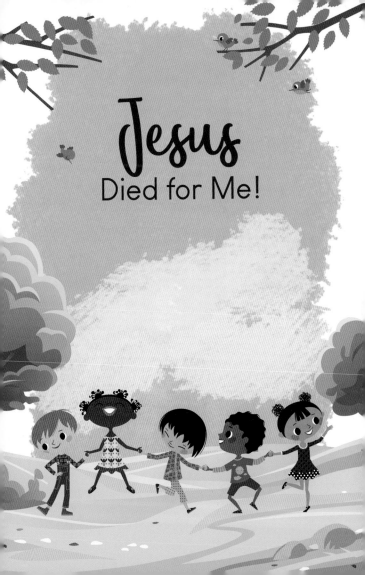

Jesus
Died for Me!

They brought Jesus to a place called Golgotha (which means "Place of the Skull"). They offered him wine drugged with myrrh, but he refused it.

Then the soldiers nailed him to the cross. They divided his clothes and threw dice to decide who would get each piece.

Mark 15:22–24

At noon, darkness fell across the whole land until three o'clock.

Mark 15:33

[Jesus] said, "It is finished!" Then he bowed his head and gave up his spirit.

John 19:30

Alleluia!

Jesus Is Alive!!

The angel said, "Don't be alarmed. You are looking for Jesus of Nazareth, who was crucified. He isn't here! He is risen from the dead! Look, this is where they laid his body. Now go and tell his disciples, including Peter, that Jesus is going ahead of you to Galilee. You will see him there, just as he told you before he died."

Mark 16:6–7

[Jesus] said, "Peace be with you. As the Father has sent me, so I am sending you." Then he breathed on them and said, "Receive the Holy Spirit."

John 20:21–22

"Why are you frightened?" [Jesus] asked. "Why are your hearts filled with doubt? Look at my hands. Look at my feet. You can see that it's really me. Touch me and make sure that I am not a ghost, because ghosts don't have bodies, as you see that I do."

Luke 24:38–39

I Will Live

Forever

This is the way to have eternal life—to know you, the only true God, and Jesus Christ, the one you sent to earth.

John 17:3

I live!

I live forever!

Because of Jesus!!

If Christ has not been raised, then your faith is useless and you are still guilty of your sins. . . . But in fact, Christ has been raised from the dead. He is the first of a great harvest of all who have died.

1 Corinthians 15:17–20

Let me reveal to you a wonderful secret. We will not all die, but we will all be transformed!

It will happen in a moment, in the blink of an eye, when the last trumpet is blown. For when the trumpet sounds, those who have died will be raised to live forever.

And we who are living will also be transformed.

1 Corinthians 15:51–52

Loving God,

Loving Others

Everyone knows that you are obedient to the Lord. This makes me very happy. I want you to be wise in doing right and to stay innocent of any wrong. The God of peace will soon crush Satan under your feet. May the grace of our Lord Jesus be with you.

Romans 16:19–20

Therefore, go and make disciples of all the nations, baptizing them in the name of the Father and the Son and the Holy Spirit. Teach these new disciples to obey all the commands I have given you. And be sure of this: I am with you always, even to the end of the age.

Matthew 28:19–20

We are looking forward
to the new heavens
and new earth he has
promised, a world filled
with God's righteousness.

2 Peter 3:13

There is more than enough room in my Father's home. If this were not so, would I have told you that I am going to prepare a place for you? When everything is ready, I will come and get you, so that you will always be with me where I am.

John 14:2–3